My United States

Rhode Island

NEL YOMTOV

Children's Press®
An Imprint of Scholastic Inc.

Content Consultant

James Wolfinger, PhD, Associate Dean and Professor
College of Education, DePaul University, Chicago, Illinois

Library of Congress Cataloging-in-Publication Data
Names: Yomtov, Nelson, author.
Title: Rhode Island / by Nel Yomtov.
Description: New York, NY : Children's Press, an imprint of Scholastic Inc., 2018. | Series: A true book | Includes
    bibliographical references and index.
Identifiers: LCCN 2017049405 | ISBN 9780531235782 (library binding) | ISBN   9780531250914 (pbk.)
Subjects: LCSH: Rhode Island—Juvenile literature.
Classification: LCC F79.3 .Y66 2018 | DDC 974.5—dc23
LC record available at https://lccn.loc.gov/2017049405

Photographs ©: cover: Mira/Alamy Images; back cover bottom: Tim Clayton/Corbis/Getty Images; back cover ribbon: AliceLiddelle/
Getty Images; 3 bottom: BookyBuggy/Shutterstock; 3 map: Jim McMahon/Mapman ®; 4 left: Eric Isselee/Shutterstock; 4 right:
Osoznaniejizni/Dreamstime; 5 top: marion faria photography/Getty Images; 5 bottom: Andrew Burgess/Shutterstock; 7 center
top: Tim Laman/Getty Images; 7 top: Ed Hughes/Courtesy Audubon Society of Rhode Island; 7 center bottom: LEE SNIDER PHOTO
IMAGES/Shutterstock; 7 bottom: Allan Wood Photography/Shutterstock; 8-9: Cate Brown/Robert Harding Picture Library; 11 back-
ground: marion faria photography/Getty Images; 11 inset: USCG/Wikimedia; 12: Kevin Fleming/Getty Images; 13: Yiming Chen/Getty
Images; 14: Shobeir Ansari/Getty Images; 15: Darlyne A. Murawski/Getty Images; 16-17: Andre Jenny/Alamy Images; 19: North Wind
Picture Archives; 20: Tigatelu/Dreamstime; 22 left: grebeshkovmaxim/Shutterstock; 22 right: grebeshkovmaxim/Shutterstock; 23 top
left: Osoznaniejizni/Dreamstime; 23 bottom right: Photography by STEVE ALLEN/Alamy Images; 23 center right: Andrew Burgess/
Shutterstock; 23 bottom left: Nature and Science/Alamy Images; 23 top right: Eric Isselee/Shutterstock; 23 center left: lissart/Getty
Images; 24-25: Stocktrek Images, Inc./Alamy Images; 27: Print Collector/Getty Images; 29: Stock Montage/Getty Images; 30 bottom
right: Giovanni da Verrazzano on the river Hudson, Scarpelli, Tancredi (1866-1937)/Private Collection/© Look and Learn/Bridgeman
Images; 30 bottom left: Stocktrek Images, Inc./Alamy Images; 30 top: Stock Montage/Getty Images; 31 top left: North Wind Picture
Archives; 31 top right: Wisconsin Historical Society/ WHS-27950; 31 bottom: grebeshkovmaxim/Shutterstock; 32: Onne van der Wal/
Getty Images; 33: Pictorial Parade/Getty Images; 34-35: Douglas Mason/Getty Images; 36: Andrew Snook/Icon Sportswire/Getty
Images; 37: JeffG/Alamy Images; 38: John Burke/Getty Images; 39: Tom Stewart/Getty Images; 40 inset: Rusty Hill/Getty Images; 40
background: PepitoPhotos/iStockphoto; 41: David H. Wells/Getty Images; 42 top left: Metacomet (colour litho), English School/Private
Collection/Peter Newark Pictures/Bridgeman Images; 42 top right: GL Archive/Alamy Images; 42 bottom right: Henry N. Jeter/New York
Public Library; 42 bottom left: Randy Duchaine/Alamy Images; 43 top: Pictorial Press Ltd/Alamy Images; 43 center: Bettmann/Getty
Images; 43 bottom left: Archive PL/Alamy Images; 43 bottom right: Kris Connor/Getty Images; 44 bottom: Kurt Deion/kurtshistoric-
sites.com; 44 top right: pederk/Getty Images; 44 top left: mauritius images GmbH/Alamy Images; 45 center: David Klepper/AP Images;
45 top right: Dina Rudick/The Boston Globe/Getty Images; 45 top left: Chee-onn Leong/Dreamstime; 45 bottom: lissart/Getty Images.

Maps by Map Hero, Inc.

Front cover: Castle Hill Lighthouse
Back cover: Beach polo players in Newport

Welcome to Rhode Island

UNITED STATES

Rhode Island

Find the Truth!

Everything you are about to read is true *except* for one of the sentences on this page.

Which one is **TRUE**?

T or F Most Rhode Islanders work in agriculture and fishing.

T or F Rhode Island's state tree is the red maple.

Rhode Island
FN-434
Ocean State

Find the answers in this book.

3

Contents

1 Land and Wildlife

2 Government

THE BIG TRUTH!

Violet

What Represents Rhode Island?

Harbor seal

4

Castle Hill Lighthouse

3 History

4 Culture

Rhode Island
Red chicken

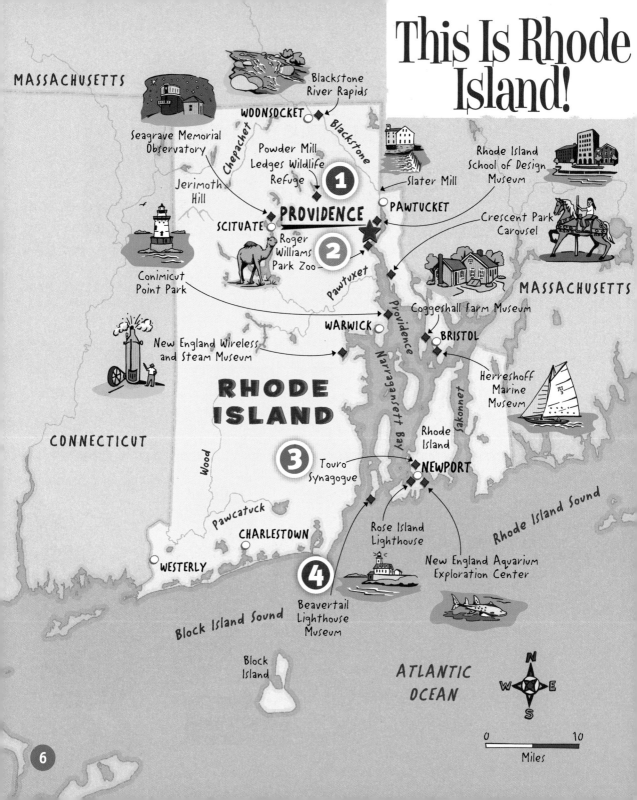

This Is Rhode Island!

MASSACHUSETTS

Blackstone River Rapids

WOONSOCKET

Seagrave Memorial Observatory

Chepachet

Blackstone

Powder Mill Ledges Wildlife Refuge

Rhode Island School of Design Museum

Jerimoth Hill

Slater Mill

1

Crescent Park Carousel

SCITUATE

PROVIDENCE

PAWTUCKET

Conimicut Point Park

Roger Williams Park Zoo

2

Pawtuxet

MASSACHUSETTS

Coggeshall Farm Museum

Providence

New England Wireless and Steam Museum

WARWICK

BRISTOL

Herreshoff Marine Museum

RHODE ISLAND

Narragansett Bay

Sakonnet

Wood

Rhode Island

3

Touro Synagogue

NEWPORT

CONNECTICUT

Pawcatuck

CHARLESTOWN

Rose Island Lighthouse

Rhode Island Sound

WESTERLY

4

New England Aquarium Exploration Center

Beavertail Lighthouse Museum

Block Island Sound

Block Island

ATLANTIC OCEAN

N W E S

0   10
Miles

① Powder Mill Ledges Wildlife Refuge

The woodlands of this 120-acre (48-hectare) property in Smithfield are home to deer, owls (pictured), wild turkeys, and dozens of types of wildflowers and trees. Visitors can hike the trails that run through the refuge.

② Roger Williams Park Zoo

Founded in 1872, this is the country's third-oldest zoo. It contains more than 160 animals, including elephants, giraffes, snow leopards (pictured), and more.

③ Touro Synagogue

Built in 1763, Touro Synagogue in Newport is the oldest Jewish house of worship in the United States. It was built by the **descendants** of Jews from the island of Barbados in the Caribbean Sea.

④ Beavertail Lighthouse Museum

Located at the entrance to Narragansett Bay, the museum tells the history of Rhode Island's lighthouses and their keepers. The 64-foot (20-meter) Beavertail Lighthouse, built in 1749, stands next to the museum.

Rhode Island has more than 400 miles (644 kilometers) of coastline.

CHAPTER 1

Land and Wildlife

As the smallest state in the country, Rhode Island—the Ocean State—is not a very large place. But despite its size, it is a state rich in history, scenic beauty, and wildlife. One of the original 13 **colonies**, Rhode Island is the birthplace of religious freedom in the United States. Its dozens of glistening, sandy beaches attract visitors from all around the world. Rhode Island is a place you have to "sea" to believe!

The Ocean State

Rhode Island measures 48 miles (77 km) from north to south and 37 miles (60 km) from east to west. Massachusetts forms the northern and eastern borders of Rhode Island. To the west is Connecticut. The Atlantic Ocean forms the state's southern border. Rhode Island has more than 30 islands. But despite its name, most of its land is not an island. The mainland of the Ocean State is divided into two regions: the Coastal Lowlands and the Eastern New England Upland.

This map shows the higher (orange) and lower (green) areas in Rhode Island.

Keep a Light Burning

Rhode Island has more than 400 miles (644 km) of coastline. To serve as an aid to ships at sea, the state has a number of active lighthouses scattered along the coast. The lighthouse towers are constructed of wood, brick, or stone. One of the most famous is the Ida Lewis Lighthouse in Newport Harbor. Established in 1854, it is no longer in service. The lighthouse was named in honor of Ida Zoradia Lewis, who served as the lighthouse keeper for 32 years!

Ida Lewis

Castle Hill Lighthouse has been active for more than 125 years.

Perched on a tiny island in Narragansett Bay, the famous Clingstone house, built in 1905, has survived countless storms and hurricanes.

The Coastal Lowlands cover the eastern part of Rhode Island. The region is made up largely of beaches, **lagoons**, and saltwater ponds. Rhode Island's three major rivers—the Pawtuxet, Blackstone, and Providence—run through the lowlands. The state's islands are located in Narragansett Bay.

The Eastern New England Upland stretches through the northern and western parts of the state. Forests, valleys, rocky hills, and lakes and ponds are found here.

Climate

Rhode Island often experiences cold winters and hot, wet summers. Providence, the state's capital and largest city, has an average temperature of 37 degrees Fahrenheit (3 degrees Celsius) in January and 83°F (28°C) in July. Powerful storms called nor'easters sometimes slam into Rhode Island and bring heavy snowfall. In February 1978, a historic storm dumped 40 inches (102 centimeters) of snow on some parts of Rhode Island and killed 26 people.

MAXIMUM TEMPERATURE
104°F

MINIMUM TEMPERATURE
-28°F

Winter storms in Rhode Island usually drop only an inch or two (2.5 or 5 cm) of snow, but the occasional nor'easter can leave several feet.

Plants

Forests cover about 60 percent of Rhode Island. Hardwood trees such as ash, hickory, maple, and walnut grow in the state's upland regions. In fall, visitors come to see the leaves of these trees turn bright red, yellow, and orange. In summer, colorful wildflowers such as violets, irises, goldenrod, and asters dot the landscape. Along the coastline, cordgrass, cattail, bluestem, and other plants thrive in wet areas.

The changing leaves of Rhode Island's forests provide breathtaking views in the fall.

Ducks gather on a frozen pond in Providence's Roger Williams Park.

Animals

Black bears, deer, rabbits, foxes, and raccoons live in Rhode Island's forests. Otters, beavers, and ducks inhabit the state's waterways. Sharks, seals, whales, tuna, and many species of shellfish live in the ocean waters off the coast. More than 400 varieties of birds soar through the skies above the state. Robins, blue jays, sparrows, and owls are common in wooded areas, while seagulls, terns, gulls, and ospreys live on the coast.

The Independent Man statue weighs more than 500 pounds (227 kilograms).

CHAPTER 2

Government

Rhode Island's capitol is located in Providence. Built between 1895 and 1904, the building is made of white marble and more than 15 million bricks. On top of the capitol's dome is an 11-foot-tall (3 m) gold-covered statue called Independent Man. The statue represents the ideas of freedom and independence that the colony of Rhode Island was founded upon.

Government Basics

The government of Rhode Island is divided into three branches: executive, legislative, and judicial. The governor is the head of the executive branch. This branch oversees government agencies and proposes the state budget. The legislative branch, or General Assembly, consists of the Senate and the House of Representatives. Its job is to make Rhode Island's laws. The judicial branch hears court cases and decides if state laws are legal.

RHODE ISLAND'S STATE GOVERNMENT

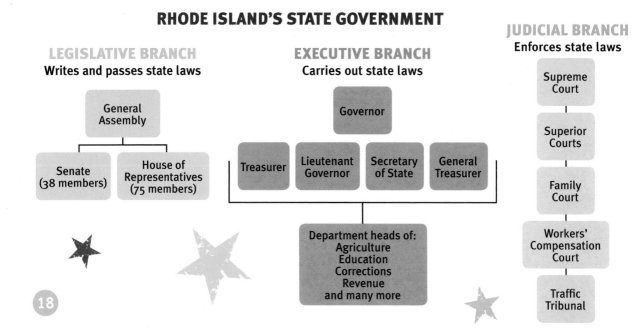

LEGISLATIVE BRANCH
Writes and passes state laws

- General Assembly
  - Senate (38 members)
  - House of Representatives (75 members)

EXECUTIVE BRANCH
Carries out state laws

- Governor
  - Treasurer
  - Lieutenant Governor
  - Secretary of State
  - General Treasurer
- Department heads of:
  Agriculture
  Education
  Corrections
  Revenue
  and many more

JUDICIAL BRANCH
Enforces state laws

- Supreme Court
- Superior Courts
- Family Court
- Workers' Compensation Court
- Traffic Tribunal

The State Constitution

The organization of Rhode Island's government and laws is spelled out in the state's constitution. This document also outlines the

In 1843, Rhode Island became the first state to grant voting rights to African Americans.

basic rights granted to the people of Rhode Island, such as trial by jury and freedom of the press. Rhode Island's first constitution went into effect in 1843. Over the years, many **amendments** have been made to Rhode Island's constitution.

Rhode Island's National Role

Each state elects officials to represent it in the U.S. Congress. Like every state, Rhode Island has two senators. The U.S. House of Representatives relies on a state's population to determine its numbers. Rhode Island has two representatives in the House.

Every four years, states vote on the next U.S. president. Each state is granted a number of electoral votes based on its total number of members in Congress. With two senators and two representatives, Rhode Island has four electoral votes.

2 senators and 2 representatives

4 electoral votes

With four electoral votes, Rhode Island's voice in presidential elections is below average compared to other states.

The People of Rhode Island

Elected officials in Rhode Island represent a population with a range of interests, lifestyles, and backgrounds.

Ethnicity (2016 estimates)

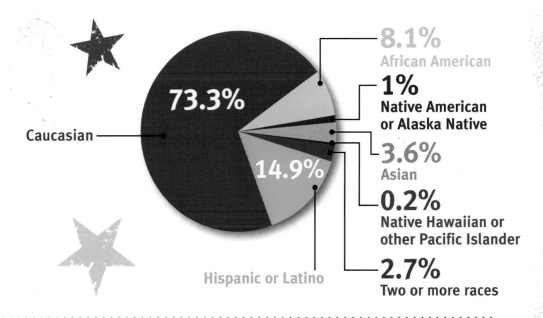

73.3%
Caucasian

8.1%
African American

1%
Native American or Alaska Native

3.6%
Asian

0.2%
Native Hawaiian or other Pacific Islander

2.7%
Two or more races

14.9%
Hispanic or Latino

20% of Rhode Islanders are under the age of **18**.

32% have a bachelor's degree or higher.

60% own their own homes.

22% speak a language other than English at home.

87% graduated from high school.

13% were born in another country.

What Represents Rhode Island?

States choose specific animals, plants, and objects to represent the values and characteristics of the land and its people. Find out why these symbols were chosen to represent Rhode Island or discover surprising curiosities about them.

Seal

Rhode Island's state seal shows a golden anchor with the word "Hope" above it. The outer circle reads, "Seal of the State of Rhode Island and Providence Plantation 1636." Providence Plantation was the colony's original name when it was founded in 1636.

Flag

Like the state seal, Rhode Island's flag features a large golden anchor. The anchor sits on a white background, and a blue ribbon with the word "Hope" in gold letters appears beneath it. Thirteen gold stars representing the original 13 American colonies form a circle around the anchor and ribbon.

Violet

STATE FLOWER

The violet was chosen as the state flower in 1968, making Rhode Island the last state to adopt an official state flower.

Harbor Seal

STATE MARINE ANIMAL

Found along the Rhode Island coast, this variety of seal can grow to about 6 feet (2 m) long and live up to 30 years.

Rhode Island Red

STATE BIRD

This breed of chicken was developed in Rhode Island in the late 19th century.

Red Maple

STATE TREE

During the fall, the leaves of this beautiful tree brighten Rhode Island forests as they turn gold, purple, and bright red.

Rhode Island Greening Apple

STATE FRUIT

Developed in Rhode Island in the late 1700s, this crisp, yellow-green fruit keeps its sharp taste in cooking.

American Burying Beetle

STATE INSECT

This endangered beetle was chosen as a state symbol to promote awareness of its need for protection.

Early people in Rhode Island used handmade spears and other weapons to hunt.

CHAPTER 3

History

About 80,000 years ago, huge **glaciers** covered the area that would become Rhode Island. As they moved, the icy glaciers carved waterways around Narragansett Bay in eastern Rhode Island. They also carried stone and dirt. As the weather warmed, the glaciers melted, leaving the landscape we know today.

The first humans arrived in the region about 10,000 years ago. These ancient people were the **ancestors** of modern-day Native Americans.

Native Americans

By the 1600s, about 30,000 Native Americans lived in the Rhode Island region. The Narragansett were the largest group. They lived west of the bay that was later named for them. The Wampanoag lived east of the bay and on many of its islands. The area was also home to smaller communities, including the Niantic, Pequot, and Pawtuxet peoples. Most groups in the region spoke the Algonquian language. Groups who spoke this language are called Algonquian people.

This map shows some of the major tribes that lived in what is now Rhode Island before Europeans came.

The Algonquian lived mostly in dome-shaped houses called wigwams. They were made by covering wooden frames with animal skins and straw mats. The Narragansett often built longhouses, which are sturdier homes made with logs and covered with bark.

Algonquian people traveled in canoes called dugouts. These boats were made from hollowed-out tree trunks.

Algonquian men pose for a photo in 1912.

Europeans Arrive

The first European to visit Rhode Island was Italian explorer Giovanni da Verrazzano in 1524. In 1620, **Pilgrims** from England established a colony in nearby Massachusetts. In 1636, a minister named Roger Williams left Massachusetts over disagreements with the leaders of the colony.

Williams bought land from the Narragansett and established the colony of Providence in present-day Rhode Island.

This map shows routes Europeans took as they explored and settled what is now Rhode Island.

Roger Williams meets with a group of Narragansett upon his arrival in Providence.

Unlike Massachusetts, Providence granted religious freedom to all faiths. The new colony thrived as its settlers farmed, raised livestock, and built small, bustling communities. In 1675, war broke out between the colonists and Native Americans. The settlers won the war the next year. Many Native Americans were killed or sold into slavery. By the early 1680s, fewer than 500 Narragansett remained in Rhode Island.

The Road to Statehood

After defeating Great Britain in the Revolutionary War (1775–1783), the American colonies formed the United States. In 1790, Rhode Island became the 13th state to officially join this new country. By the early 1800s, industry, trade, agriculture, and transportation boomed in the Ocean State. During the Civil War (1861–1865), more than 24,000 Rhode Islanders fought on the side of the Union.

Timeline of Rhode Island Events

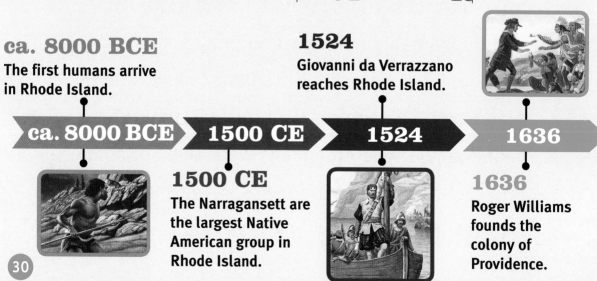

ca. 8000 BCE
The first humans arrive in Rhode Island.

1524
Giovanni da Verrazzano reaches Rhode Island.

| ca. 8000 BCE | 1500 CE | 1524 | 1636 |

1500 CE
The Narragansett are the largest Native American group in Rhode Island.

1636
Roger Williams founds the colony of Providence.

The Twentieth Century

During World War I (1914–1918), Rhode Island produced battleships, ammunition, and textiles for the war effort. Sailors trained at stations in Newport. During the 1930s, however, tens of thousands of residents lost their jobs in the **Great Depression**. When World War II (1939–1945) erupted, more than 100,000 Rhode Islanders served in the armed forces.

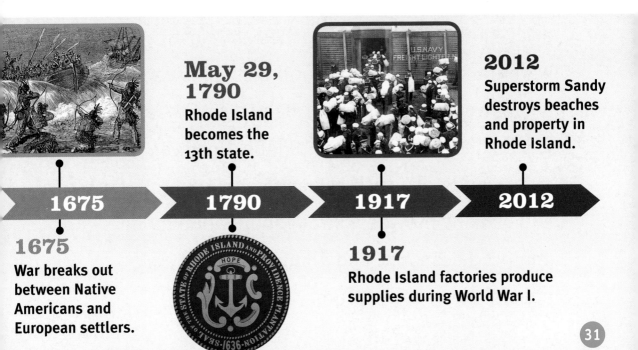

May 29, 1790
Rhode Island becomes the 13th state.

2012
Superstorm Sandy destroys beaches and property in Rhode Island.

1675   **1790**   **1917**   **2012**

1675
War breaks out between Native Americans and European settlers.

1917
Rhode Island factories produce supplies during World War I.

Hundreds of commercial fishing boats operate out of Rhode Island.

Rhode Island Today

Rhode Islanders have faced many difficulties in recent years. In 2012, Superstorm Sandy swept away large stretches of beaches and destroyed waterfront property, roads, bridges, and water and power systems. Today, many residents are leaving the state in search of jobs. However, stable industries such as health services, tourism, and banking provide a strong foundation for an improved economy, and Rhode Islanders are hopeful about their future.

A Champion of Civil Rights

Warwick's George Wiley (1931–1973) was a leading voice in the fight for **civil rights** and economic rights during the 1950s and 1960s. While teaching chemistry at Syracuse University, Wiley organized a local chapter of the Congress of Racial Equality (CORE), an influential activist group in the civil rights movement. He later founded the National Welfare Rights Organization, which fought for the rights of the poor and elderly. Today, the George Wiley Center of Pawtucket continues his work.

The Newport Jazz Festival draws huge crowds to Newport for live music each August.

CHAPTER 4

Culture

Rhode Island makes up for its small size with a thriving arts and culture scene. The state's many museums feature outstanding exhibits of Native American arts and crafts, early American history, transportation, and much more. Newport is home to grand 19th-century mansions that attract visitors from around the world. Concert halls and theaters offer world-class local and international music, dance, and drama performances.

Let the Games Begin!

Rhode Island has no major professional sports teams. However, sports fans support the state's minor league teams, such as the Pawtucket Red Sox (baseball) and Providence Bruins (hockey).

Rhode Island's waters are ideal for yachting and boating. The state's seashore, forests, cliffs, and parks offer plenty of opportunity for hikers, campers, and other lovers of the outdoors.

Each year, the Hall of Fame Tennis Championships are played in Newport.

Floating bonfires light up Waterplace Park in Providence during a WaterFire event.

A Blazing Work of Art

Rhode Island hosts a variety of annual celebrations. Providence, the state's capital, dazzles locals and tourists with a series of events called WaterFire. On certain nights, about 100 sparkling bonfires are anchored in the three rivers that pass through the city. As they watch the crackling flames, visitors stroll along the river, listening to enchanting music and watching performing artists. Millions of people attend the lightings each year.

A craftsman in the town of Wakefield works on a handmade custom guitar.

Making a Living

About 80 percent of Rhode Islanders work in service industries such as health care, tourism, real estate, education, and finance. Providence and Warwick are home to the headquarters of many large banks and insurance companies. Many people work in manufacturing. Hasbro, one of the world's largest toy manufacturers, is based in Pawtucket. The company is famous for toys, which include G.I. Joe and Transformers action figures.

A commercial fishing crew sorts through its catch near the coast of Rhode Island.

Wonderful Water

Rhode Island has a huge fishing industry. Lately, the state's fishers have had to respond to a number of legal and environmental changes. Government officials have placed limits on the number of certain fish that can be caught. Different patterns of fish **migration** have also affected the industry. To combat these changes, people are fishing for different species. For example, Jonah crabs are now caught in Rhode Island to support the shrinking lobster industry. More fish farms have also been established. At the farms, fish are raised in tanks or sealed-off areas.

Let's Eat!

It's only natural that Rhode Island has a reputation for great seafood. Mouthwatering lobster ravioli, crab cakes, clam chowder, and fried calamari (squid) are local favorites. People also enjoy doughboys, which are made from sweet, fried dough. Breakfasts often feature johnnycakes, small cornmeal pancakes smothered with butter and maple syrup or molasses.

★ Rhode Island Grinder

Ask an adult to help you!

This beloved sandwich is popular throughout the Ocean State. It's tasty and a cinch to make!

Ingredients

Italian bread
Olive oil
Red wine vinegar
Sliced onions and tomatoes
Shredded lettuce

Slices of provolone and mozzarella cheese
Slices of hard salami, Italian ham, and pepperoni

Directions

Slice the bread. Brush olive oil and red wine vinegar on the inside of two slices. On one side, place a layer of onions and then a layer of tomatoes. Add lettuce. Layer with the cheeses and meats. Press the sandwich together and slice in half at an angle. Rhode Island restaurants often leave the sandwich open and put it under a broiler until the cheese melts.

See It to Believe It!

Rhode Island is a land of natural beauty and rich history. It has thundering surf and miles of glistening sandy beaches. Whether you're a longtime resident or a first-time visitor, the state has an incredible variety of things to do. Take the Cliff Walk along Newport's rocky coast and marvel at the breathtaking views of the sea. Enjoy a horseback ride on one of the state's many trails. Visit the Audubon Society in Smithfield to get a firsthand look at fascinating wildlife habitats. You'll never run out of things to see in Rhode Island! ★

Famous People

Metacomet

(ca. 1638–1676) was a tribal leader of the Wampanoag Nation. He fought a bloody war against English settlers before being killed in a final battle.

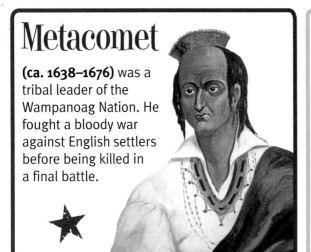

Gilbert Stuart

(1755–1828) was one of America's greatest portrait painters. His most celebrated work is the unfinished 1796 painting of George Washington. He was born in Saunderstown.

Elizabeth Buffum Chace

(1806–1899) was influential in the antislavery movement of the 19th century. In later years, she fought for women's rights and better conditions in prisons and the workplace.

Revered Mahlon Van Horne

(1840–1910), was a pastor and politician who in 1885 became the first African American to serve in the Rhode Island General Assembly. He lived in Newport.

Matilda Sissieretta Joyner Jones

(1869–1933) was an opera singer who performed for several U.S. presidents and the British royal family. Born in Virginia, she moved to Providence as a child.

Raymond Hood

(1881–1934) was an architect who worked in the art deco style in the 1920s and 1930s. His most celebrated buildings include Rockefeller Center and the McGraw-Hill Building in New York City and the Tribune Tower in Chicago. He was born in Pawtucket.

Louis B. Mayer

(1884–1957) was a film producer and co-founder of Metro-Goldwyn-Mayer (MGM) movie studios. Born in Russia, he moved with his family to Rhode Island as a child. Under his guidance, MGM produced many classic movies, including *The Wizard of Oz* and *Gone With the Wind*.

H. P. Lovecraft

(1890–1937) wrote strange, eerie fiction, and developed a devoted following with stories such as *The Lurking Fear*, *The Rats in the Walls*, and *The Mystery of the Graveyard*. He was from Providence.

Dee Dee Myers

(1961–), a native of North Kingston, was the first woman to serve as White House press secretary. She held the position during the administration of President Bill Clinton. She is a best-selling author, writing mainly on women's issues, politics, and the media.

Did You Know That . . .

Founded in 1747, the Redwood Library and Athenaeum in Newport is the oldest library building in continuous use in the United States.

The first public roller-skating rink in the United States opened in 1866 in the Atlantic House, a resort hotel.

Nine Men's Misery in Cumberland is the oldest monument to veterans in the United States. Erected in 1676, it honors nine colonists killed by Narragansett Indians during the region's violent war.

Rhode Island is home to several colleges and universities. Among the most famous are Brown University and the Rhode Island School of Design. Both are located in Providence.

Newport is home to the International Tennis Hall of Fame, located in the Newport Casino, an athletic and recreation center built in 1880.

The Flying Horse Carousel in Westerly is the oldest carousel in the United States still operating in its original location.

The world's largest model of a bug sits atop the roof of Big Blue Bug Solutions in Providence. Known as Nibbles Woodaway, the giant blue termite is 9 feet (3 m) tall and 58 feet (18 m) long, and weighs 4,000 pounds (1,814 kg)!

Did you find the truth?

F Most Rhode Islanders work in agriculture and fishing.

T Rhode Island's state tree is the red maple.

Resources

Books

Burgan, Michael. *Rhode Island*. New York: Children's Press, 2015.

Felix, Rebecca. *What's Great About Rhode Island?* Minneapolis: Lerner Publications, 2015.

Petreycik, Rick, Lisa M. Herrington, and Hex Kleinmartin. *Rhode Island: The Ocean State*. New York: Cavendish Square, 2015.

Rozett, Louise (ed.). *Fast Facts About the 50 States: Plus Puerto Rico and Washington, D.C.* New York: Children's Press, 2010.

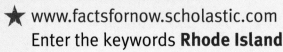

Visit this Scholastic website for more information on Rhode Island:

★ www.factsfornow.scholastic.com
Enter the keywords **Rhode Island**

Important Words

amendments (uh-MEND-muhntz) changes that are made to a law or legal document

ancestors (AN-ses-turz) members of your family who lived long ago, usually before your grandparents

civil rights (SIV-uhl RITEZ) basic rights guaranteed to all citizens, such as the right to vote and the right to equal treatment under the law

colonies (KAH-luh-neez) communities settled in a new land but with ties to another government

descendants (dih-SEN-duhntz) your descendants are your children, their children, and so on into the future

glaciers (GLAY-shurz) slow-moving masses of ice formed when snow falls and does not melt because the temperature remains below freezing

Great Depression (GRAYT dih-PRESH-uhn) a worldwide economic crisis that took place mostly during the 1930s

lagoons (luh-GOONZ) shallow bodies of water separated from the sea by a reef

migration (mye-GRAY-shuhn) movement of people or animals from one region or habitat to another

Pilgrims (PIL-gruhmz) the group of people who left England because of religious persecution, came to America, and founded Plymouth Colony in 1620

Index

Page numbers in **bold** indicate illustrations.

About the Author

Nel Yomtov is an award-winning author who has written nonfiction books and graphic novels about American and world history, geography, science, mythology, sports, science, careers, and country studies. He is a frequent contributor to Scholastic book series.